From Fear to Hope
&
Back Again

Jose Acosta

Writers Club Press
San Jose New York Lincoln Shanghai

From Fear to Hope & Back Again

Published by Writers Club Press
an imprint of iUniverse.com, Inc.

For information address:
iUniverse.com, Inc.
620 North 48th Street, Suite 201
Lincoln, NE 68504-3467
www.iuniverse.com

ISBN: 0-595-12949-8

Printed in the United States of America

Dedication

To those that know of Fear and dream of Hope, and those that know of Passion.

Contents

List of Illustrations

Front Cover: Organ Mountains, Las Cruces, New Mexico
Thanks to the City of Las Cruces for their courtesy in the use of the cover photograph.

Preface

After reviewing the manuscript to this book, I found myself reflecting on the many emotions and events that have created and formed the man that I am today. Life is so full of many memorable times. Even the darkness of the world makes the sunshine seem so much brighter. As does the lack of love make a simple kiss so special. This collection of poetry is a gathering of my memories. All come together in the sequence of my life. Not all memories are good ones, but all have shaped the adult I have become. The person one becomes, I believe is influenced greatly by the experiences and emotions of their youth. We are not given a choice of our childhood, therefore, we can only learn from it. I have tried to express those experiences in poetry.

This book may come as a shock to many that do not know of my childhood. For I have hidden what happened to me for over 35 years. I sometimes wanted to shout from the highest hills and let the world know my anger. Yet, sometimes I want to cower in a corner and take my last breath and know life no more. Abuse is a crime that last a lifetime, not only a few seconds or hours. It is relived in the memories and flashbacks of victims. The effects are felt as a person grows and this experience of abuse forms the way a person deals with emotions throughout their life.

This book is also of hope. The kind love has shown me. From the innocence of a child giving a father a hug, to the warmth of kiss from a woman. All these I dealt with, with compassion and sometimes fear. I have not dealt with emotions with the greatest of compassion and I know of many that have suffered due to my ignorance. To those I apologize. I have placed the writings in this book in sequential order that would reflect my life. Perhaps a novel would have been a better way to write and tell my story. Perhaps, but I have found that poetry has allowed emotions to flow easier in the many times memories have overcome me. The title, "From Fear To Hope & Back Again", reflects the roller coaster ride of emotions an abused person goes through. Even when life seems the best and love seems to be in abundance, flashbacks can reduce one back to childhood and one can become as helpless and hopeless as the child once again. A friend that was abused as a child and kept it a secret read my work and told me that ti was so real it brought tears. Another person read "Amidst the Morning Sun" and said it was as strong as the love and emotions her husband shared. Those words encouraged me to put this book together. Love has a strong presence in my life, but sometimes those nights and times when solitude lets the mind drift and open the doors for memories. In those instances a man can become that child again. From that point of view I have written some of my work. I have a passion for life, I always will and hope that passion is reflected in my writing.

I

From Fear...

The First Day

Sitting on a shinning floor,
creased pants never worn before.
Ice cream sweet, teardrops not,
smiling people seem so a blur.

Scents so clean, so new to me,
small clutching hand hangs on.
As my smaller brother leans,
looking for dad, sis or mom.

Matching plates with matching cups,
social worker plump and stern.
Shakes man's hand, evil smile,
waves good by and leaves alone.

Don't offer me a blanket warm,
sobs from brother as I him hold.
Don't reach for us, just go away,
no tears from me, I am too damn old.

Leave us to cry, let us to pray,
oh Father, whom to you I turn.
A child of five, with heart sheared,
where are we now? Inside I burn.

My brother's tears have torn my soul,
my parents home is not now known.
Why this clothes, why new shoes,
why ice cream sweet, where is my home?

Was I so bad at being a kid,
was I so cruel to my mom and dad?
Why do I sit on a cold shining floor?
why does my brother seem so sad?

Where have my siblings gone,
where did all the love depart?
Why do I sit here holding him,
how do I mend his broken heart?

I know of praying at times like this,
from a frightened child hear I pray.
Send me those Angels I hear about,
help my family, they took away.

This house of matching colors,
smiling woman and happy man.
I want not gifts or socks of new,
we're lost, don't try to understand.

Upon a new bed we are taken to lie,
with a quilt of patches soft sewn in.
With the setting sun darkness comes,
tears now can rush out from within.

A Boy at Five and Fear

Your touch has never left my soul,
your face imprinted in my mind.
Your wetness lingers strongly still,
in memories fresh and not so kind.

The fiery redness of your hair,
your voice, hands cold as ice.
Awaken me in the darkest hours,
clawing innocence with each slice.

Naked vision of your skin so white,
freckled with red spots of fire.
Stood haunting as you raped my soul,
my body, to satisfy your sick desire.

A child at five I was many years ago,
when as an adult you crossed me.
Even now at thirty-nine I fear,
nightmares so real that wake me.

One day upon some ground I'll stand,
above a grave where you'll lay deep.
I'll bow and pray and ask the Lord
to burn your soul so I may,
sleep.

Country Miles

Country miles, rows of corn,
unknown paths run by friends.
Slowly does the scene turn dark,
for horror here never ends.

Walls covered with puzzles and glue,
as to hide the ghosts of children past.
Quilts made with care and colors bright,
all false visions, joy does not last.

Closets dark, leather straps,
screams at night not heard so far.
As evil does enter the room,
a child hopes on a falling star.

Angels turn their back again,
as tears of pain do fall.
For innocence of a kid is broken,
against a cold and bleeding wall.

Crumbled down lies a shell,
of a kid once full of love.
As angels cry in sweet lament,
one soars in sorrow from above.

In arms of golden wings he wraps,
a heart so small to even know.
The reason for the pain and hurt,
or why a child is treated so.

Ceremonial cloth and verses too,
whispered by a man of GOD.
No audience to hear the sound,
as a lonely mother tosses sod.

In the distant a siren wails,
another child from man's pain.
As darkness descends upon the earth,
angels tears fall like acid rain.

God is Somewhere

God is somewhere in the room,
a child in silence cries.
His warmth and love will ease,
pain, fear and love that dies.

Angels supposedly watching him,
as bruises come in black and blue.
Their wings of gold to comfort me,
as tears of blood from do flow.

God is somewhere in this room,
a child in prayer again screams.
God's love will conquer all,
even the painful midnight dreams?

A torn child lies to die,
as fists were swung in rage.
no heart, no love, no breath,
as life turns its final page.

yet they say again,
God is somewhere in this room.

Hymns, Hope Then Fear

A church, a candle, a soothing hymn,
now praises and cheers for all to hear.
Hold hands, sing louder, joy is felt,
their is only love, no sign of fear.

Stained glass, an altar, a peaceful hug,
we exit the door, a passing glance.
The car, the smell, such emptiness,
no love, no hope, not one chance.

A seat belt, the breathing, the stare,
silence of tear drops one can feel.
Jesus stays in his perfect home again,
another day, night, this is real.

The road, the house, the open door,
breathing deepens, to see her smile.
Jesus doesn't live here, never did,
only pain and fear at this country mile.

Lunch, prayers mumbled, bread broken,
now darkness comes, their is no love.
A boy of five by her sickness taken,
Jesus watches safely from above.

Just No More!

No more pain,
no more screams,
no more rain.
No more falling,
no more scars,
no more living
behind bars.
No more eyes,
of black and blue,
no more nightmares
or screams at two.
There is no more,
as I lay down,
a final rest and sleep.
As my lungs exhale,
one last gentle breath,
my shattered soul invites..
the peacefulness of death.

Where Are My Angels?

Shadow eclipsing bedroom door,
my heart rapidly does race.
Small hands clenched in fear,
failing to hide a frightened face.

Scent so thick of cigars and beer,
closer the tall demon slithers in.
Dragging sounds of leather straps,
bring flashes of horror from within.

Boots of steel scratch the floor,
from my bed, sheets quickly rip.
I close my eyes and grit my teeth,
comes the lashes from the leather whip.

Oh where are those angels from church,
the ones we sing and cheer about?
That fight for children, love and hope,
where are they? My heart screams out!

Six foot five demon shouts in anger,
my wrists and arm twist in pain.
Sensations of fire cross my back,
leather scorches like acid rain.

What have I done, who did I cross,
my soul in silence does scream?
Where are my angels to stop this man,
where are my angels from a dream?

Tears with blood run to the floor,
the demon exits as I lay.
Scars may come and again go,
my heart can't stand another day.

Upon my knees I beg my Lord,
let this be my final breath.
A child of five has no hope,
please send me a peaceful death.

Then Comes the Night

With gifts, smile, many news,
they come to see our health.
With notes and queries for us,
money comes along with wealth.

New clothes, new shoes,
all these today I wear.
Good food upon the table,
show of good will to share.

We hug, we laugh, we even play,
the sun even came out so bright.
Then in their proud chariot they go,
with them they take the light.

Then comes the night,
as fiery redness show in eyes,
lust and anger overcome.
Prey cowers with silent cries.

How does a day of laughter,
fake joy and toys for smiles,
become so lost in darkness,
as fear destroys a child?

So shame does take my soul,
silent screams no one to hear.
For day was light and joy..
but anger & hate brought fear.

Then comes the Night.

Voices Scream

Voices scream
as I crouch,
in a corner of my room.
Words so sharp
cut through my heart,
as two that I love do yell.
Thinness of the walls,
let pain and fear come in.
Voice scream as in tears,
I sit
in a corner of my room.
a child cries.

Another Whipping

A whipping for a too-loud whisper.
Another for a sock left on the floor.
A cursing that cuts the soul for making,
a noise, when closing a simple door.
Dark closets like isolated cells.
Clenched fists to fight back tears.
Cold water upon a face to hide,
swollen lips and blackened eyes.
Threats of being put to the streets.
So many nights with hunger fallen,
to sleep on a cold bare tiled floor.
To believe one's worthlessness as told.
But the pain that made all so minor,
the words never spoken or heard.
The lack of love, hope or kindness,
Sheared a heart forever more.

A Child's View of Life

Serenity..
Security..
Honesty..
   So hard to reach,
   so hard to understand,
   so hard to find.
Tears of pain fall on barren ground,
from the eyes of a torn soul abused.

Faith..
Hope..
Love..
   Distant thoughts,
   failed dreams,
   betrayed by hearts.
Broken souls not heard do cry,
another night of darkness arrives.

Warm embraces..
Self confidence..
Sweet dreams..
   Flashes of fear replace,
   harsh words do deepen wounds,
   dreading night, sleep does come.
Nightmares so real in sweat awake,
as horror grasps a young soul again.

Life..
Happiness..
Death..

One is long with pain,
  one is short with staying,
    death seems like peaceful sleep.
So whisper wishes of good times,
of love unknown, of faith gone by,
one child in dark despair does cry.

Among the Candles

Scented candles, amber lights,
Shadowed statues, solemn eyes,
Pews of oak, polished clean.
Thickness of air, lingers in.
Take the host, drink the wine.
Sins forgiven in one silent swipe.
Tears fall from those who believe,
with arms raised to embrace the sky.
A child kneels among the crowd,
Hands clenched tight in prayer said.
Among the coldness of the saints of stone,
a broken heart in silence cries.
Only to be drowned in praises sung.
Deepening stares from angels painted,
among the walls of this hallowed church.
No one hears the child's soul scream,
as one more tear falls from a blackened eye,
From a cross a solemn tear is shed to see,
pain, of a child screaming and yet not heard.

A Survivor's Plea

So senseless the days are passing,
so strong the urge to want to die.
As if my heart can break no more,
I sit in solitude, breakdown and cry.

Laughter of children to sad to hear,
my soul awaits a mournful night.
Tears of blood flow with sorrow,
across a heart sheared with fright.

Ghosts of memories dark with horror,
as claws reach deeper into my mind.
Devour flashes of joy and happiness,
leave scarring nightmares behind.

Too many nights end like this one,
many screams from past I hear.
As shadows do awake my senses,
as a child again darkness I fear.

Upon a Summery Day

How fresh the roses smell,
on such a summery day.
Grass so green feels alive,
as in it I look up and lay.

Coolness of the running water,
soothes my bare young feet.
Birds do sing and frolic,
as the earth and I do speak.

Suddenly the sun darkens,
a voice of HIM I hear.
Shadow of a man so tall,
brings sudden instant fear.

Birds seem to fly away,
waters become dead still.
Grass cuts into my soles,
as I am taken against my will.

Standing in frozen emotions,
so young so small, no love.
Words so harsh they slice my soul,
from the man who stood above.

No reason for the yelling,
no reason as every night before.
Alcohol needs not a conscience,
to throw a child against a door.

Emptiness fills my heart,
tears from me no longer run.
Bruises on my skin might go,
but my broken soul has one.

Sickening smells of spirits,
beer, wine fill the air.
In a puddle of loneliness I sit,
no one really to care.

Curse the Gods, brought the wine,
the keeper of the bars.
Curse the minister that states,
"All will be fine, pray to the stars."

How do you mend a broken home?
How does a child stop a mom that cries?
How can you say this world is good,
as another abused child dies?

A Late Farewell

Smell of alcohol and cigars stale,
vomit drying on restroom floor.
Eyes swollen red from fallen tears,
another hole in a beaten door.

Approached my bed with horrid breath,
I faced the wall to not look back.
To apologize as the night before,
sighing to see, my eye was black.

I hate the smell of cigarettes,
I get sick at the odor of any beer.
For what he did broke my soul,
at 39, I still wake in fear.

This time I come to him in his sleep,
to see those eyes so cold and still.
Hands so big have shrunk with years,
of whose pain in dreams I often feel.

A blackened rose, I place on his chest,
sign the cross, kneel to hear no breath.
This man I loved and hated so,
my father, I now celebrate his death.

Broken Dreams, Fallen Tears

Shadows against a pool hall wall,
cigarettes and beer fill the air.
Cheap whiskey mixed with tired souls,
broken dreams seem so unfair.

Carpet full of stains unknown,
waitress with a painted smile.
Time passes as does hope,
each step seems a longer mile.

In a distant home a woman cries,
silent tears as supper cools.
Beauty faded by hope gone by,
as games of men are played by fools.

Night does fall on broken homes,
shattered love causes fears.
Shadows long with sorrow show,
lonely sheds fallen tears.

J J

To Hope...

Was it your kiss?

Was it your kiss,
that awakened me
from life so bare of love?

Was it your touch,
that made me feel,
passion once I knew of?

Was it your breath,
so warm and gentle,
upon my skin so cold?

Was it your kiss,
that brought such life,
to a shattered darkened soul?

It was all these,
for now I know.
love upon me did breathe.

In your hand I place,
My heart.
for all you did so give.

First Emotions

Smiles that say so much,
Quick glances that so entrance.
Warm waves of emotions,
From hearts sent out.
do capture feelings,
from,
a new romance.

Visions of lips so smooth,
seem to say,
passion does await.
Skin as soft,
as waters warm it seems,
Enticing innocent,
tempting
dreams.

Romance at Sunset

Sitting on the soft sands of a isolated beach,
Hearing the soft melody of the crashing waves.
In awe of the beauty of the setting sun as it blended
In the horizon of the oceans edge,
I breathed in the crispness of the fresh air.

Even the slight mist felt cool to my skin.
As the soothing rays of the leaving sun caressed me,
once more to savor the loveliness of nature,
to be enveloped in such splendorous view, I could
not think of a more wonderful feeling of tranquility.

Then your hand touched mine, as you placed
your head on my shoulder, I melted.
As love once more,
overcame me, the sun dispelled its final days light,
we kissed.
Nature bows at the sight of such romance.

You Took My Breath Away

You took my breath
away today,
by the closeness
of your lips.
My mind went off,
just wondering.
Oh, how sweet,
would be your kiss.
You took my breath
away today,
when you merely said,
"Hello".
Thoughts of passion
long forgotten,
rushed as waves,
upon a shore.
You took my breath
away today,
When our bodies
briefly touched.
Your beauty,
so inspired dreams of want,
just thought,
that you should know.

Melody of Passion

In the middle of the night,
The melody of your heartbeat woke me.

Sitting there I caressed the softness of your skin,
felt the warmth of your breath upon my chest.

Seeing the peacefulness beauty of your face,
I sighed and embraced you.

And like a dream, I drifted to sleep again.
As our spirits flew hand in hand to touch,

the innocence of the clouds and feel the rush
of the wind from eagle's wings,
we kissed.

Engulfed in the sweet passion of love,
I smiled and held you tighter and closer.

Thanking the heavens and earth for the love,
time, and passion we do so share.

When Did You?

When did you
enter my mind to stay?
Your vision
consumes my thoughts.
As youthful desires,
dance in dreams,
to savor a kiss yet to be.
When did you
first warm my heart,
that once knew only,
pain?
To think, to want, to see
you near.
Yet never have
lips yet to kiss.
When did you comfort,
a soul so empty?
With a smile to say,
hello.
You enter the room,
my heart does sigh,
perfume I savor so,
Your walk,
your smile,
your tender eyes.
How do you
pan flames of passion?
How you do,
excite me so.
For when you did,

Upon my life so
breathe,
a fire deep
from sparks
did glow.

Envious of the Sun

Did you feel the sun caressing you?
I so do envy its every ray.
To touch upon such velvet lips,
to gaze upon your lovely face.
So as the ocean's mist,
lies softly upon your skin,
I dream of sweet emotions,
As when passion engulfed our dreams.
So know my dear,
the evening breeze,
that enters your room at night,
carries a kiss so gentle,
I have placed upon the wind.
For in dreams we dance and find,
flight as high as eagles dare.
Reaching heights of ecstasy,
from memories
we do both share.

Rain so Lovely

Gentle rain against my window,
scent so fresh across the sky.
Sweet and soft it falls on roses,
Showering a gliding butterfly.

Your lips of red I do vision
as soft as that fallen rain.
Caressing me with passion,
washing away all my pain.

Roses grow from nourished waters,
strengthened by the love and sun.
so does my soul from your kisses,
to melt with you, to become one.

Never have I seen one so lovely,
whom chased away my fears.
With innocence, love and laughter,
with one touch you wiped my tears.

Lay gently down on pillow of grass,
now birds do sing me to sleep.
Dreaming once more of your kiss,
in solitude I softly weep.

It Was You

It was your hand,
I held so gentle,
your first breath,
that gave me life.
It was your skin so soft,
your hands so small,
your scent so sweet,
my child I held,
that first night.

It was your voice,
your first words,
the mumbling did cheer,
my once darkened life.
It was your hand,
I held to see you step.
My child I saw,
hope in your eyes.

It was your pictures,
of trees, circles and squares.
It was your many "why's",
that did so take my heart,
and gave me life.
It was your face,
your strength of soul,
your kindness I felt,
it was your tears,
that broke me down.
It was you my son,

that gave me life,
forever more.

Breathing

Softly across velvet lips so smooth,
warmth of passion from inside.
Deepened by desire found,
again to taste a kiss.
Embraces blend souls in love,
heartbeats in unison do sing.
Two lovers meet on clouds
of lust,
to breathe emotions, wants
and dreams.
Two hearts ignite,
as flames erupt,
even angels stop to sigh.
Romance so true breathes again,
as lover's spirits fly.

Love Emotions

The earth shook today,
But there was no movement.
A gentle breeze touched me,
but there was no wind at all.

Sweetness of honey I tasted,
but never was there food.
Felt the softness of a cloud,
but the skies were clear and blue.

All this I felt as our lips did meet,
with one touch I felt a kiss from you.

A Touch, A Kiss

Tingling feeling overcame me,
memories so warm in thoughts.
Glance that sends chills abound,
kiss so gentle as a whisper.

To hold a hand and touch,
the warmth of your skin.
To say love without words
embracing as the world vanishes.

For this is love in purity,
of innocence and beauty.
Heartbeats beat together,
as two rush to arms of love.

Not charred by hurt or pain,
nor blurred with deceit or doubt.
This love I feel for you is real,
a gift from as an angel sent to me.

Now sleep my love tonight,
as in my arms I hold you.
My heart can feel your pulse,
as we melt with one last kiss.

Without a Word

I heard you say "I love you"
though you never said a word.
I felt it in the kiss you gave.
The warmth of your touch

Surrounded by scent of roses,
your head rest on my chest.
Wetness of a warm rain caressed me,
we kissed and loved the night away.

I heard you say "I love you",
and you never said a word.

Passion for Love

Lights dimmed in room of shades,
as night does come once more.
Satin sheets with pillows wait,
anxiousness makes heart a glow.

Simple touch so warm so tender,
a kiss says love without voice.
Bodies blend, melt with desire,
passion erupts in lover's flames.

Mouths do meet in heat and fire,
breathes so deep quickly taken.
So strong the rasping of emotions,
as two, to unknown heights arise.

Ecstasy overcomes each other,
shivers felt as both surrender.
Inhaling rare lust and desire,
pleasure found in form of want.

Slowly do the warm waters calm,
soothing caresses, tender felt.
With love came hunger to wander,
among the souls of two in love.

Soft Shadows

Soft shadows from a midnight moon,
stars gently caress her face.
Warm breezes from ocean comes,
as lovers gasp, fall to embrace.

Waves of heat engulf each one's mind;
touches send sparks to souls afire.
Warmth of breath, wet with want,
bodies consumed by sheer desire.

Mouths meet as hearts ignite,
fires of heat as legs entwine.
Emotions high as eagles' flight,
ecstasy flows as sweet red wine.

Each kiss deeper, two become one,
now on clouds these spirits lie.
Nor sun, nor moon can be as bright,
as lover's flames light up the sky.

Resting in arms and post emotions,
holding tight to this blessed dance.
Earth and heaven smile in envy,
at the sight of true romance.

So Close We Sit

Sitting so close,
I can feel you breathe.
Initiating visions so sweet,
as to savor,
our first kiss.
To dream of embraces soft.
My heart enveloped
with thoughts so tender.
Emotions stirred.
How close we sit.
Swirling with emotions,
excited with youthful dreams.
So close I feel
your heartbeat,
and taste your breath.

A Morning Kiss

To place a rose upon your pillow,
to gently kiss your cheek.

To see your face being caressed,
by the rays of the morning sun.

The warmth of your loving hug,
as your lips touch my skin.

As departing hands are felt,
emotions stirred in loving hearts.

Every breath taken by your beauty,
My soul is blessed with your love.

For you my angel, are my life,
my passion, my desire, my want.

And as the morning breeze comes in,
A thankful man departs,
with love on his mind.

Amidst the Morning Sun

As a distant drum,
beats in a valley low,
birds do whisper songs.
Two hearts do blend in melody,
lovers welcome the dawn

Tender touches soft,
rays of light come in,
caressing skin so sweet.
Again for lips to taste,
warmth, as souls do meet.

Entwined as vines,
merged as one,
passion does a heart race.
Bodies blend, to take again,
of ecstasy in love's embrace.

Arms strewn with strength,
breast as soft as warm rain.
Hands clutch each one in lust.
Both do inhale breaths so deep,
while waves of heat and bodies thrust.

Two lovers melt,
two dreamers sigh.
Souls as high as eagles fly to dance.
Two hearts beat as bodies blend,
wrapped in wings of sweet romance.

I Need to be Kissed

I need to be kissed.
To feel the breath,
leave my lungs in ecstasy,
to savor the warmth of your mouth,
Feel the wave
of emotions flow,
from your lips overcoming my heart.
To close my eyes
when we embrace,
absorbing every moment of passion.
I need to be kissed.
As if were the first
time we felt,
the desire, the want, the love.
I miss the look in your eyes,
when we held each other
with post emotions of love,
seeing you fall asleep in my arms,
to dream of eternity being so sweet.

Fear Does Leave

In me there is fear.
In me there is hope.
In me there is longing,
and most of all,
there is love.
Just waiting for an
arm to embrace it.
But against the darkest clouds,
I stand to let my child,
touch my hand,
then all the fear,
all the longing,
and solitude disappear.
As the chill of loneliness
leaves in shame.

Two Lovers Blend

Warmth of body, soul and heart,
we touch.
Lips aflame with passion found,
we kiss.
Silhouettes of lovers dance,
we embrace.
Ecstasy and lust become one,
we love.
Flames as high as angel's flight,
we surrender.
Heartbeats in melody do sing,
we sigh.
Emotions wrapped by hearts afire,
contented spirits dream.

When I Bring You Roses

If I send you roses,
will they be enough?
Can they wipe the tears,
that fell last night like rain?
Can flowers bring forgiveness,
to a heart blurred with pain?

Can petals soft,
caress your skin,
as I would like to do again?
Can the colors red and velvet,
bring love back once more?
If I send you roses,
can I be the deliverer at your door?

So when I bring your roses,
As they blush upon your hand.
I wish for them,
to take away the strife.
For when I bring you roses,
let them be a sign
of love for life.

III

&
Back Again

Death of Innocence

Innocence was killed today,
a headline read again.
A child died of rage unknown,
as others outside played.
Tears fell on barren ground,
an infant's last breath taken.
Anger took a life today,
as angels wept,
and parents lied.
A small soul to heaven taken,
as God's wrath again held back,
Thunder roared, and rains did come.
a shallow grave for broken bones,
again to hide the shame.

Yesterday's Thoughts

From atop building,
a view so vast and beautiful.
The sun so close, it's warmth
caressing my very soul.
The ground so green and
far below.
How can a world so lovely,
create so much pain?
One slip, one fall,
to end the tears,
that can't be seen.
To stop a heart,
that can no longer feel.
To stop a mind that
thinks too much,
even among the confusion.

Perhaps my spirit will fly,
from the ground as I fall.
To soar as free as eagles.
to hurt from love no more.

Then a flash,
my child's kiss,
the soft touch of
her hand.
Not even heaven has
such sweet emotions.
I step back,
to return to life,

to hold my precious
child.
In tears of confusion,
I once again feel,
the beating of my heart.

Memories from a Child

Flashing memories brought to mind,
chills of fright and pain.
Flush with heat of anger comes,
slashing down like sharpened rain.

Hopelessness into my soul,
sunken feeling in my heart.
Hands do shake as cold arrives,
memories please from me depart.

Tears of a child held back again,
in a corner in my mind I hide.
For shattered dreams do overcome,
a child comes out, from inside.

How does one stop such flashes?
How can one hurt a child's soul?
Where were angels that solemn day,
when evil in my life did go?

Even time has not diminished,
horrors of a time gone by.
For even a man at thirty-nine
becomes a child, sits to cry.

No way to stop emotions,
nor tears that fall and pool.
Shame overcomes my face,
I sit, helpless like a fool.

Breath of Wings

Was not the breeze, woke my soul,
around the mid of night.
Was not the soft sweet rain,
brought upon the chills of fright.

Still was the air, bore no wind,
dry was the evening skies.
It was at midnight that I felt,
lips gently kiss my sleeping eyes.

No winged bird made the flutter,
whose breath touched my heart.
Nor was the moon that shone in blue,
visions of love that did once part.

From my sleep a voice did speak,
with the kindness of an angel's tone.
"Be not afraid, be not alarmed my love,
for you will never, never be alone."

A tear did flow down my cheek,
my heart sank as there I lie.
For now I knew Heaven had my angel,
in solitude and loneliness I cry.

Now when the rains come gently down,
caressing my skin and face,
breathe the air and feel the warmth,
to the heavens my arms do raise.

To touch her once, to feel her skin,
to know her lips once more.
I curse the skies and thank the rain,
aching like so many times before.

So sing of hymns and praises,
glorify such spirits from above.
For in your joy I cannot be,
It was those gods stole my love.

For that day when in my arms,
my beloved with her last breath,
clutched my hand, as tears fell,
welcomed the painlessness of death.

Say no more to me of love,
say no more to me of dreams.
Till the day when with her I wake,
I shall feel the breath of wings.

A Love Remembered

Rain softly beats upon my window,
thunder roars in distant skies.
Dreaming of days we walked together,
with love reflecting in your eyes.

Drops fall, caressing flowers,
clouds being shaken from above.
Again my mind drifts to your kisses,
swirling with memories of our love.

With the wind the storm is gone,
a rainbow shines across the sky.
As to say the Lord has you darling,
I miss you, I pray, and bow my head,
to cry.

Too Late, Too Gone

Sun sets, darkness approaches,
once more the moon comes to cry.
Stars seem as splattered tears,
across the saddened midnight sky.

Shadows long, deep with sorrow,
cover ground that once was green.
Dove's voices sang in melancholy,
blackened hearts silently scream.

A heart full of love now is empty,
too late, too gone for to say.
Ghosts of past embrace his soul,
He awaits
another mournful lonesome day.

Illusions

An awakening chill
crawled up my spine.
As a morning breeze
came upon me.

Was it your touch
from your spirit's hand,
come to say hello?

Again I felt,
this time the warmth,
as beams of sunlight
touched my lips.

Your kiss I felt
as so many times before,
in dreams of passion past.

A heart so void
since we did part,
creating illusions of emotions.

How much emptier
is a soul,
after once caressed by love.

When Did Love Leave?

When did love leave our house?
Was I asleep when it did part?
When did your touch turn so cold?
Words so sharp can freeze a heart.

Where did all the passion go?
Where did beauty's love fly?
The love we both felt and saw,
what day, what night did it die?

My desire never left.
My wanting you remained.
Your warm breath upon me,
feelings so strong are still the same.

No love, no passion only pain,
emptiness and lonely nights.
Shadows split against the wall,
lovers once now regretting rites.

Where did our passion go?

Clear Bottles

Beneath our bed lacking love.
against a corner of a closet full.
Smaller in a dresser drawer,
clear with labels of unknown names.

One way screams for reasons not.
Love drowned in spirits high.
Words stronger than vodka white,
cuts a heart with shattered dreams.

Shaking hands in morning reach,
with apologies for forgotten rage.
Darkened windows to hide the sun.
noon arrives, reach for bottles saved.

Hope left with the setting sun,
once again darkness fell.
Bottles clear come to call,
helplessness hits the floor.

Demons in a Corner

Happiness stays not long,
in minds when darkness comes.
Setting suns and moonlit nights,
leave hope at dusk and dawn.
Peacefulness, joy and love,
cower in a corner of one's mind.
Flashes from fear devour,
dreams of hope thought to stay,
while men fall to knees, women do pray.
Each in own one's way succumbs to fear,
all abused in rage, so many years,
A pill,
a couch,
a tranquil thought.
Remedies by readers of minds,
forget the darkness of a soul.
For there a child in a corner lies,
waiting for demons to again arise.

In Solitude

Why does solitude awaken a heart?
Why do tears not wash away pain?
How can loneliness mean so much,
after love did fall as sweet rain?

Does a broken heart ever mend?
Does a spirit lose all hope to fly?
Can one ever again open up a heart,
when as now with tears does cry?

Is there an honest soul on earth?
Has love departed with the sunset?
For when love left, darkness fell,
broken hearts in solitude have wept.

An Angel's Kiss

An angel came to kiss me last night,
Its wings caressed me as I lay.
Scent so sweet of perfume I smelled,
"I love you" its gentle voice did say.

Then in the silence of its departure,
loneliness, emptiness came once more.
As tears upon my bed again did fall,
leaving me in solitude as I was before.

I woke to clutch a photo of love gone,
my breath, my world to soon left.
realizing that the kiss, the angel,
was you as in shadows, I wept.

What Would I Miss?

The softness of your kisses,
the warmth of your breath.
The smile of my baby girl,
the hugs from my sons.

The sun rays caressing my face,
the colors of a rainbow .
The sweet crisp smell of the sea,
the tiny voice of an "I love you".

Can heaven be so sweet?
Can it erase my longing for you?
Is there something softer than,
the tenderness of your touch?

Oh death that does come so quickly
with promises of a better life.
Have you seen the sparkle of,
my child's eye in the morn?

Can you tell of a better love,
when you have not felt the touch?
When my child reaches for me in darkness,
or as to my arms she does rush.

Let me wait another day,
to breathe the morning air.
Feel the crisp breeze of the ocean,
to cherish every rose I see

Lord, one more day on this earth,
for I love what you have given me.
And so do cherish every moment here.
One more day, one more kiss.

One more reason to say thank you,
before I go to your arms, I pray.

Color of Sadness

If sadness had a color,
would it be blue?
For tears are clear,
and love is gone.
What color is sadness?
As loneliness brings,
in the darkness,
of a love lost.

My heart cries out in solitude,
to only be heard,
by the winds amongst the mountains.
As lonely spirits fly,
my spirit lies on fallen snow.
Bitter with cold,
and emptiness of soul.

No touch can overcome,
or warm the broken heart.
For tears dripped on darkened dreams,
create a deeper river of despair.

Once Again to Dreams

Never a day passes by,
when a tear for you falls not.
Never a day shall come to me,
when in solitude I do not cry.

For as the roses parade in bloom,
or birds in melodies do sing.
The winds of time stop to say,
love ends not with death or spring.

To reach the skies, touch your soul,
to taste of love once past.
Close my eyes, breathe again,
and back to dreams that last.

Again our spirits dance above,
like when we did embrace.
A day or thousands moons go by,
still for you my heart does race.

Upon the wings of eagles' I send,
a kiss, a touch so tender.
To let you know forever more.
our love I shall remember.

I'm Note a Rose

I'm not a rose,
for I do not fade.
I'm not a rose,
beauty is my soul.
I'm not a rose,
thorns do give pain.
I'm not a rose,
a fragile heart I have.
I'm not a rose,
these tears are not rain.
I'm not a rose,
for without love..
I die inside as only,
a shell will remain.
I'm not a rose.

Days of Love & Sorrow

Days of young past so fast,
when youth is marked with pain
Days of sun and meadows green,
darkened by sleepless nights of rain.

Days of fathers teaching children,
how to catch, draw and dream.
Days of love long forgotten,
awakened with a midnight scream.

Toys become signs of sorrow,
kisses bitter, with whisky taste.
Shaded rooms and dust filled pictures,
hope and dreams do lay to waste,

Years pass on as bruises vanish,
scars of the heart never heal.
A boy knew not love only pity,
becomes a man to hurt to feel.

A son is born as angels hover,
a sign of hope, dreams and love.
A broken man kneels to his Father,
thanking for a gift from above.

Tears of sorrow become showers,
to nourish life and wash away pain.
As the new sun rises so does hope,
as rainbow after a summer rain.

My Mom Forgot Again

My birthday is here for me to celebrate,
father, brothers, friends came late.
Even my girl came by with a card and a kiss,
everything perfect, but someone I miss.

Played with my gifts and showed a bit,
my new clothes are envied by all and fit.
Even the sun is shining and bright as to say,
"Welcome to another year and another day."

Through all the noise and music I listen,
my heart is so silently wishing.
For the phone to ring it's familiar song,
to say she'll be here and not to long.

It rings and my heart skips a beat,
it's her, now my day is complete.
She'll meet me at one at street's end,
I'll be there to show her my best friend.

I look at my dad and try not to see,
the tears he has shed for me.
When she promised to be here before,
didn't call and never knocked on the door.

Today she'll show she's not that mean,
too important to not see me turn 15.
I can't wait to see her in her new car,
in the one I'll ride with her so far.

It is ten 'till one so I must go and wait,
for my mom and our very own date.
I'll show her my shoes and gifts too,
she'll be here at least by two.

One more hug my father and don't worry
she'll come, now I must hurry.
Today is my birthday and she'll be here!
I know she promised. That I did hear.

Well. It's not long almost 2,
I'll see her new car, it's blue.
My friend has come to be with me,
he is here to keep me company.

It's 3, perhaps the traffic or the cold.
is keeping her, so I'll wait some more.
It won't be too long you'll see,
her car will drive up she'll kiss me.

Hi Dad, I know it's five,
perhaps its takes long to drive.
Maybe it takes time to go to a store,
so please let me wait a little more.

It's six o'clock and I will go in,
it's colder, she did it again.
"I love you son this is your day
a pizza, a movie, what do you say?"

Today is my Birthday we celebrate,
nobody will see me cry this late.

Soon it will be Christmas, she'll be here,
she promised when she did not show,
last year.

A Crumb

Sometimes I hate you,
so much.
Wishing we never met.
When words so cruel,
you say,
slash deep into my soul.

Always looking up I am,
at you.
Upon the pedestal I built,
for you with love and hope.
Just waiting,
for a falling crumb of compassion.

Cold Words

I walked outside barefoot,
after a quarrel.
The frozen ground
I compared to the coldness
of your words
My feet then felt warm
and the chill of the wind
did no longer bite.

Perhaps

Perhaps the wind had stopped,
The breeze stands still.
Eagles once in flight,
rest perched on limbs of high.
Perhaps the sun forgot to shine,
or fish no longer swim.
Meadows lost their luster,
of colors bright and green.
Creeks of trout no longer run,
birds no longer sing.
Perhaps,
the stillness of the earth,
was only in my mind.
Perhaps,
but still I know,
the beauty of a sunset did depart,
when you left
and in your hand you took,
my breath, my soul.
For each kiss you gave,
to me did so inspire life.

IV

Thoughts

Moving

So many things to put aside,
clothes, books.
Where did all the years go?
A crumbled paper at my feet.
Unwrapped to read the faded lines.
Heart sank so suddenly.
As words come quickly,
a bill.
Numbers.
Notes of where and when,
my younger brother's funeral.
Can't breathe so well now,
tears do overflow.
Why did you take a young man so?
Why do so dreamers die?
Good by once more,
my loving brother.
Good by my friend.

Know My Friend

I cannot feel your pain.
My tears fall for your soul.
If wings of angel's I had,
I would wrap your heart,
and keep it from the cold.

Life so precious,
children come as gold.
To fill our lives,
brighten our days,
with love we so behold.

Know my friend,
I am here for you.
As shelter in a storm of rain,
know my friend,
I will do my best,
To shroud you from the pain.

Know my friend,
your child lies,
In comfort of an angel's arm.
Know my friend,
she smiles now,
never again to know no harm.

In the Darkness

In the darkness of a corner,
in a house lacking love.
Cowers a child in a corner,
lacking hope.
In the darkness of loneliness,
a tear begins to fall.
Only to be heard as silent,
as the love down the hall.

I Didn't Even Know You

Smiles from a kid so young.
Crazy, black, wild hair.
Deep eyes of innocence,
seldom laughter, seldom cries.
Did I not see you there?

So blurred the memories,
of this child.
So deep the stare in my mind.
So many times he comes to visit,
to sit, look at the wall of mine.

With a glance from deep brown eyes,
my soul shivers from his glare.
No words are said.
Just haunted silence,
from my smaller brother sitting there.

Upon a grave,
I toss some sod.
A young man laid to rest.
The sun beats down upon my neck,
as I reach for memories, I ask God..

So many friends came to say goodbye.
A father, mother came to cry.
Passionate tears around me flow,
and all I can do,
is ask why.

We did not spend time together,
We did not laugh, cry, or stories tell.
As at your grave,
on bent knee,
I give my brother a late farewell.

A bullet struck his heart,
alone he died so far away.
No friends, no family,
to hold his hand.
Forgive us all, we did pray.

No one to blame,
no one saw him die.
The bibles says, forgive, forget.
A young man died,
he was my brother,
all I for him I did, was cry.

Adria, My Angel
(For My friend Jeff)

An emptiness I feel inside,
filled with memories of love.
Oh soul, so lonely does it cry,
as I look to you so far above.

Angels sing to comfort me,
as heaven does rain a tear.
Even angels know the pain,
the loneliness of night I fear.

Perhaps an angel listens to,
the breaking of my heart.
Perhaps one day, I pray,
God will not keep us apart.

Darkness of night does come,
as so many times before.
I lay on a bed once full of love,
to weep for you once more.

Not a day shall pass I swear,
that I will forget to send a kiss.
Let God's dove deliver one each day,
to show how much you're missed.

The Lord's Welcome
(Commander's Mom)

It is time to rest my friend,
no more pain to feel or tears to fall.

Your love has fed the world with hope,
your missions have all been met.

The garden you sowed has reaped,
the greatest of fruits, your children.

Let there not be sadness in your home,
for you come to prepare a better one.

Your faith has opened a door for your soul,
so take the hand of the Angel I sent.

Trumpets will glare and harps will sing,
for with God you will be forever more.

And as it rains upon the earth once more,
let them be tears of joy you send to say.

"I am resting now in the arms of the Lord,
so smile my children, live and do pray,

For there is no pain or sadness in heaven,
for I see and feel only love forever more".

It is time to rest my beloved friend
so leave your pain at my door.

Your Smile I Miss

So many times you smiled,
you laughed,
you ran,
you took my hand.
So many times I held you,
you hugged,
you kissed,
you loved with innocence.
So many times while I was at sea,
you inspired,
you empowered,
you danced in my mind.
Now only a memory,
of a child full of hope,
of tears that fell,
or a heart so small,
and broken.
Like lightening and as sharp,
strong as the voice of thunder,
you enter my mind,
you bring back days we shared.
Nights of loneliness,
you filled with love,
nights of despair,
you gave hope to fear.
You never left my mind,
even now,
so many years have past,
I miss you,
and wish you the best.
my first and lovely son.

My Neighbor

To be like the neighbor.
Bored with simplicity.
Excited for a friendly card game.
Content with a morning kiss goodbye.
Comfortable with stability.
Greatest fear,
rainstorm after a car wash,
I envy that man.

Aboard a Vessel Far

Tranquility of waves that dance,
horizons peak and fall.
Illuminating lights below,
as currents flash at night.
Come out the stars, again to say,
sailor rest and dream.
Set down your worries,
calm be your soul.
Your vessel's safe upon the sea.
Giant engines hum a song,
Power yearning to be released.
Shadows eerie from guns at rest,
reminder of Freedom's costly price.
Dolphins do come to play,
against the wake that follows.
Friends of the seas,
bring peaceful thoughts,
as nature and man do speak.

Teardrop falls,
from a seasoned sailor,
clutching a photo of a child.
So strong the love left at port,
so strong the love desired.
Closer to heaven,
one does not get,
as when at sea at night.
For there, God's hand
embraces man.
As those ashore,

in peace do rest,
warriors dream of loves on land.

The Price of Freedom

So many shouts against our FLAG,
so many screams of hate and rage.
As with their freedom they do yell,
against the wars of past present days.

A flame erupts among the crowd,
Red, White and Blue does burn.
More shouts by those so naïve,
to blind, to young to ever learn.

Then in the midst a soldier stands,
with medals pale with time and pride.
Scars of wars on his face do show,
upon a steel chariot he does ride.

"Know you not of men that died,
of women sent to early graves.
As for your freedom they did stand,
so many heroes so many braves.

Rows of stones with forgotten names,
proud soldiers laid to peaceful rest.
Did die for that FLAG you so burn,
with their life they gave their best."

Silence came upon the raging crowd,
as this soldier stood in pain,
He rendered one more sharp salute,
as heaven's angels came.

A broken heart stopped that day,
too much for one to silently bear.
Memories of friends past that fell,
so strong the past so still unfair.

So if you do not know the price,
of freedom you do so use to rave.
Look beneath at yonder rows of stone,
for that price they Proudly gave.

A proud Veteran.

Love Has Hues?

Born a babe.
Named a name.
Given clothes,
without shame.

Grew to be,
child of five.
School brings kids,
with staring eyes.

Hair is black,
never bothered me.
Now it seems,
means inferiority.

Levi's jeans,
no big deal.
Others wore,
insults I feel.

Smiling girl,
eyes so blue.
Touches hand,
likes me too.

Hair not black.
Heart is gold.
Feelings strong,
"Don't" I'm told.

Silent whispers,
friends advice.
Weeps and leaves,
didn't look twice.

Broken hearts,
young and pain.
Love has no color,
neither does rain.

Tell me why,
tears have no hue.
Nor does passion,
why then, why do you?

Each Loving Memory

Was I there when you cried?
Did your heart my warmth?
Not one tear fell that I did not catch,
to wipe with love, compassion,
and understanding.

For each memory,
each moment spent in your arms,
I weep to feel the emptiness,
of my soul.
And envy every angel,
whose eyes gaze
at your beauty,
savor your very voice.
And so flourish in the love
you so brought to heaven.

Death of Innocence

Innocence was killed today,
a headline read again.
A child died of rage unknown,
as others outside played.
Tears fell on barren ground,
an infant's last breath taken.
Anger took a life today,
as angels wept,
and parents lied.
A small soul to heaven taken,
as God's wrath again held back,
Thunder roared, and rains did come.
a shallow grave for broken bones,
again to hide the shame.

Printed in the United States
3430